THE APACHE

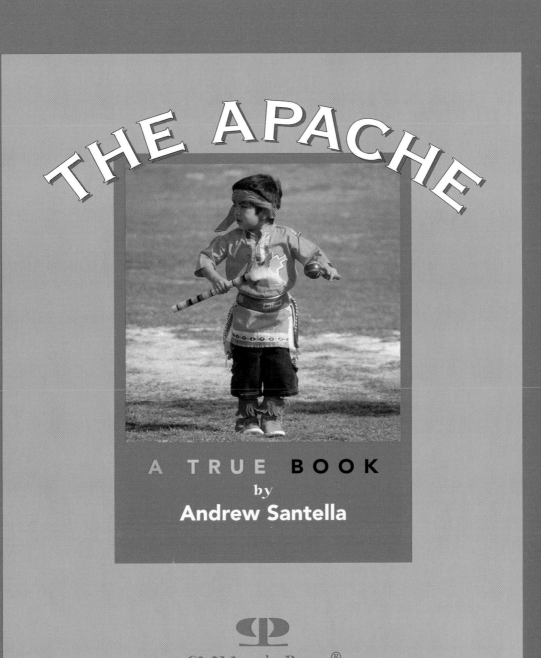

A TRUE BOOK

by
Andrew Santella

Children's Press®
A Division of Grolier Publishing

New York London Hong Kong Sydney
Danbury, Connecticut

A statue on the San Carlos Apache golf course

Reading Consultant
Lane Roy Gauthier
*Associate Professor
of Education
University of Houston*

*The photograph on the cover
shows an Apache girl riding her
horse in Whiteriver, Arizona.
The photograph on the title
page shows an Apache boy
performing a traditional dance.*

**Visit Children's Press® on
the Internet at:
http://publishing.grolier.com**

Library of Congress Cataloging-in-Publication Data

Santella, Andrew.
    The Apache / by Andrew Santella.
       p. cm. – (A True book)
    Includes bibliographical references and index.
    ISBN 0-516-22215-5 (lib. bdg.)   0-516-27311-6 (pbk.)
       1. Apache Indians—History—Juvenile literature. 2. Apache Indians—
Social life and customs—Juvenile literature. [1. Apache Indians. 2.
Indians of North America—New Mexico.] . Title. II. "True book" series.

E99.A6 S35 2001
979.004'972—dc21   00-024013

1 2 3 4 5 6 7 8 9 10 R 10 09 08 07 06 05 04 03 02 01

Contents

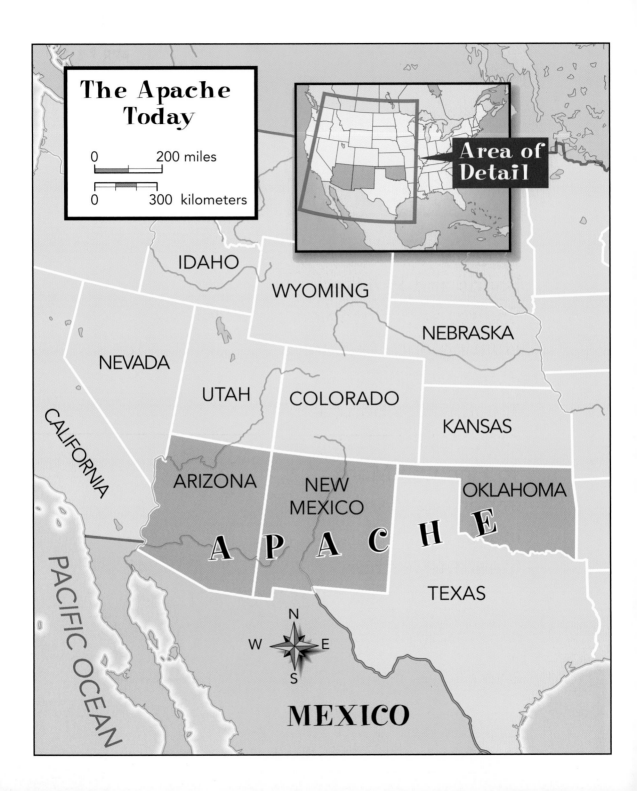

The Apache
Today

0   200 miles

0   300 kilometers

Area of
Detail

IDAHO

WYOMING

NEBRASKA

NEVADA

UTAH   COLORADO

KANSAS

CALIFORNIA

ARIZONA   NEW
MEXICO

OKLAHOMA

A P A C H E

TEXAS

PACIFIC OCEAN

N
W   E
S

MEXICO

Origins

About one thousand years ago, a group of North American Indians in the icy northwestern corner of Canada began looking for a new home. They traveled south along the Rocky Mountains. Hundreds of years later, this group made their way to what is now the southwestern United States.

No one knows for sure why they moved. They may have been searching for new sources of food. After all, the Apache were nomads. Nomads are people who move from place to place in search of food or a better climate.

The Apache adapted to their new home. It was hot and dry—very different from their old home. They had always been hunters, but soon they learned new skills. The

Apache learned to live off the plant and animal life in the Southwest. They also learned to farm and make pottery. The members of other tribes in the area probably taught them.

The Apache became very warlike. They invaded their neighbors for food, livestock, and weapons. The Apache became the most feared group in the Southwest. The Zuni (ZOO-nee) people, who

An Apache Indian by Frederic Remington
shows an Apache warrior defending his home.

also lived in the Southwest, called them apachu, or "enemy." That is the origin of the name Apache. The Apache have a different name for themselves. They call themselves n'de, or "the people."

Bands and Families

Over many years, the Apache spread all across the Southwest. They formed six separate groups: the Mescalero (mes-kuh-LER-o), Jicarilla (hee-kuh-REE-yuh), Lipan (li-PAN), Chiricahua (chir-uh-KAH-wuh), Kiowa (KIE-uh-wah) Apache, and

A Chiricahua Apache princess

Western Apache. Each group had its own language, customs, and traditions. But the languages were similar enough that they could understand each other. All Apache saw themselves as a unified people.

The Apache were organized into bands. Each band was made up of several extended families. The extended family included cousins, aunts, uncles, parents, and grandparents.

Mothers played a very important role in Apache families. When a man and a woman married, they lived with his wife's family. When a man returned from hunting, he brought the food to his mother-in-law.

Shelter and Clothing

Apache bands lived in camps. In the camps, some Apache lived in tepees. A tepee is made of a frame of wood poles that are tied on top to form a cone. The tepee's frame is covered with animal hides.

Other Apache tribes lived in wickiups (WI-kee-ups). A wickiup

A tepee covered with animal hides (left) and wickiups in an Apache village (above)

is made of thin sticks bent over and tied at the top to form a dome. It is covered with grass or leaves. The Apache kept a fire going inside the wickiup for warmth and cooking. A hole was cut out of the top to let smoke escape.

Apache wore simple clothing for the hot, dry climate of the Southwest. Men wore a loincloth that hung from the waist to the knees. Women wore buckskin skirts. Both men and women wore knee-high moccasins with hard soles. The toes of the moccasins curled upward. The Comanche

The moccasins of an Apache woman

(kuh-MAN-chee) people called the Apache ta-ashi, or "turned up," because of their moccasins.

Hunting and Gathering

Apache kept moving from place to place to hunt and gather food. They hunted deer, rabbits, elk, and other animals. Apache who lived on or near the Plains hunted buffalo.

At first, Apache hunted with bows and arrows. Later,

they hunted with guns. Sometimes, Apache used other strategies to trap small animals such as rabbits. Large groups of Apache would form a circle around the animal. Then they would walk toward each other, making the circle smaller and smaller. If the animal tried to escape, the Apache would catch or club it.

The hunters brought back meat that was roasted, boiled, or raw. Sometimes, the

Apache laid meat out to dry on racks. When it was dried, the meat lasted longer. They cut the dried meat into long strips and ate it like jerky.

Women gathered wild fruit, vegetables, roots, and nuts. Piñon (pin-YONE) nuts were an important part of the Apache diet. They are found in the cones of pine trees that grow in the Southwest. The nuts were ground up for flour or eaten whole.

Piñon nuts

Apache also ate the leaves of mescal plants—a kind of cactus. They baked the mescal leaves in stone ovens. This plant was so important that the Mescalero tribe was named after it.

An Apache
woman gathering
corn on a farm

Some Apache tribes also
farmed. The Western Apache
were considered the best
farmers. They grew corn,
beans, and squash.

Apache Fiddle

The fiddle is a traditional musical instrument of the Apache. The sound box of the Apache fiddle is made from the stalk of a yucca plant. It holds a single string that is attached to a tuning peg. It can be tuned like a guitar. It is played with a bow made of animal muscle.

Everyday Life

Apache boys and girls were expected to work hard. Boys were instructed from childhood to become hunters and raiders. Their fathers and grandfathers taught them how to make hunting weapons. The boys learned to imitate animal calls to attract the animals they

were hunting. They also learned the rules of warfare. They began joining in raids even before they were teenagers.

Girls learned to use weapons, too. Sometimes they helped hunt for small wild animals. Their female relatives taught them many skills, such as how to sew, tan hides, and gather and cook food. Girls also learned which wild plants were good to eat and which were harmful.

An Apache girl went through an important ceremony when she turned thirteen. The ceremony meant that she

Apache girls were taught many skills.

This Apache ceremony (right and opposite) is very important to teenage girls.

was ready for marriage. The girl dressed in a special costume, and older women

said prayers for her. When the
ceremony ended, her family
celebrated with a feast.

Apache

An Apache girl learns to make baskets.

Many Apache groups are known for their beautiful baskets. Apache women make baskets using skills passed down through generations. The baskets are made of fibers from plants and trees, including the yucca plant and the cottonwood tree.

Baskets

Baskets are designed for different uses. One kind of basket is lined with pitch, a sticky substance from pine trees, to make it watertight. It is ideal to use as a water jug.

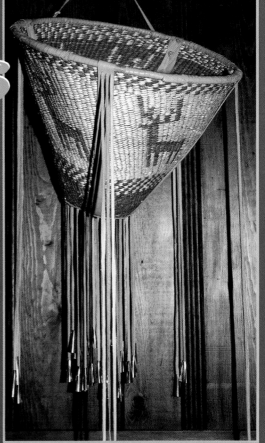

Meeting the Europeans

In the mid-1500s, Spanish explorers and missionaries arrived in the Southwest. The Apache got horses, sheep, and other European animals from the Spanish. The horses became very important because they helped the Apache travel great distances to find food and to make war.

The Apache fought hard to keep their land.

The Spanish and Apache tried to be friendly to each other, but before long, they were at war. In the mid-1800s, settlers and soldiers from the

United States tried to take control of the area where the Apache lived. The Apache fought with them, too. The Apache resisted the control of white people longer than any other tribe.

Eventually, American troops defeated the Apache warriors. The U.S. government forced the Apache on to reservations. The Apache had to change their lifestyle because they could no longer travel from place to place to hunt.

The last group of Apache to surrender to American troops was led by Geronimo (jeh-RAH-ni-moe). He was a leader of the Chiricahua tribe. For years, Mexican and American

Geronimo (first row, third from the right) and other Apache prisoners sitting outside their railroad car in Arizona

troops tried to capture Geronimo. Some rival Apache tried to capture him, too. He was captured several times, but he always escaped.

Finally, in 1886, Geronimo was captured for good. He and a group of fifty Apache were surrounded by about five thousand American troops. He told General George Crook, "Once I moved about like the wind. Now I surrender to you and that is all." Geronimo died in 1909 at Fort Sill, Oklahoma.

Apache Life Today

Thousands of Apache still live in Arizona, New Mexico, and Oklahoma. Many of them live on or near reservations. In many ways, life on an Apache reservation is like life anywhere in the United States. Children go to school, play sports such as basketball, and rent movies from the video store.

White River Apache houses (above). The Apache enjoy sports such as rock climbing (left).

Tribal councils govern Apache tribes. Tribal leaders are trying to improve the quality of life on reservations. They start new businesses to create good-paying jobs for Apache men and women. The White Mountain Apache of Arizona opened a museum to display tribal traditions. This museum is in Fort Apache, a building once used by U.S. soldiers who fought the Apache.

The Mescalero Apache in New Mexico opened a ski resort that employs many Apache. The San Carlos Apache of Arizona run a golf course. Tourists from all over the country come to ski or hike in

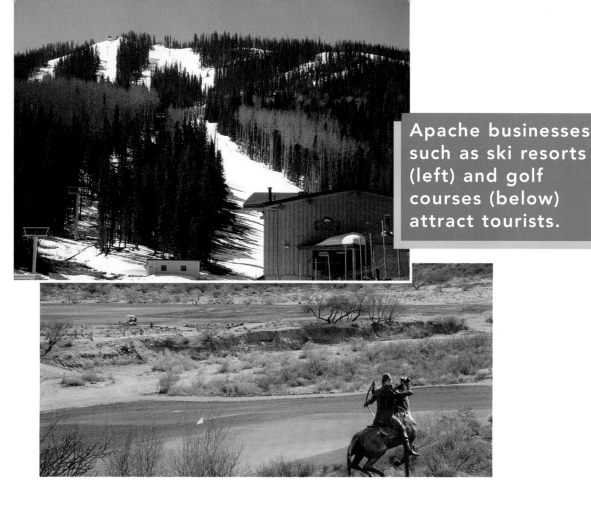

Apache businesses such as ski resorts (left) and golf courses (below) attract tourists.

the mountains and to fish in the lakes and streams on Apache reservations.

Some Apache also work as farmers or cattle ranchers. Many

others work in the timber industry. The Fort Apache Timber Company employs more than four hundred Apache. The White Mountain Apache own the company.

Many families today follow Apache traditions and customs. They practice crafts such as making baskets. They perform traditional dances to celebrate special events. Apache history and language are taught in many schools on the reservations. The Apache want to remember their proud history, but they are also working hard to create a better future.

Today, the Apache follow customs with dances, ceremonies, and traditional clothes (left). The Apache continue to build a better future for their children (below).

To Find Out More

Here are some additional resources to help you learn more about the Apache:

 **Books**

Claro, Nicole. **The Apache Indians.** Chelsea House, 1993.

Hermann, Spring. **Geronimo: Apache Freedom Fighter.** Enslow, 1997.

Lund, Bill. **The Apache Indians.** Bridgestone, 1997.

Schwarz, Melissa. **Cochise: Apache Chief.** Chelsea House, 1992.

Sneve, Virginia Driving Hawk. **The Apaches.** Holiday House, 1997.

Organizations and Online Sites

Fort Apache Historic Park
P.O. Box 628
Fort Apache, AZ 85926
*http://www.wmonline.com/
attract/ftapache.htm*

This site reveals the history
of the many structures in
the park.

**National Museum of
the American Indian,
The George Gustav
Heye Center**
One Bowling Green
New York, NY 10004
*http://www.si.edu/cgi-bin/
nav.cgi*

This site displays information on the museum's
exhibits and programs.

**Native American History
Navigator**
*http://www.ilt.columbia.
edu/k12/naha/nanav.html*

This site has maps, history,
timelines, and a search
function for students.

San Carlos Apache Tribe
P.O. Box 0
San Carlos, AZ 85550
*http://www.primenet.com/
~itca/Tribes/sancarl.htm*

This site displays a variety
of information about this
Apache tribe.

**White Mountain
Apache Tribe**
P.O. Box 700
Whiteriver, AZ 85941
*http://www.primenet.com/
~itca/Tribes/whitemtn.htm*

This site displays information on the White
Mountain Apache.

Important Words

adapt to make changes for survival in a new environment

ceremony a set of customs that mark important occasions

livestock horses, sheep, cattle, and other useful animals kept on a farm or ranch

missionary a person working to spread his or her religious faith

reservation a piece of land set aside as the home of American Indians

tan to make animal hide into leather by soaking it in a solution containing chemicals found in the bark and wood of trees

yucca a plant with spiky leaves found in warmer parts of North America

Index

Meet the Author

Andrew Santella lives in Chicago, Illinois. He is a graduate of Loyola University, where he studied American literature. He writes for a wide variety of newspapers and magazines, including *The New York Times Book Review* and *GQ*. He is also the author of several books for young people, including the following Children's Press titles: *The Battle of the Alamo*, *The Capitol*, and *The Chisholm Trail*.